ANIMALS IN WARTIME
COLOURING BOOK

Published by IWM, Lambeth Road, London SE1 6HZ
iwm.org.uk

ISBN 978-1-912423-76-7

A catalogue record for this book is available from the British Library.

Printed and bound by Gomer Press Limited
Illustrations by Frances Castle

Every effort has been made to contact all copyright holders. The publishers will be glad to make good in future editions any error or omissions brought to their attention.

www.carbonbalancedprint.com
CBP2275

ANIMALS IN WARTIME
COLOURING BOOK

Illustrations by
Frances Castle

Animals have helped in wars since ancient times, serving in many different roles along the way.

Some animals were mascots and helped people by cheering and comforting them. Others performed important jobs, like sending messages or pulling heavy supplies. At the start of the First World War armies grew to enormous sizes, and the number of animals needed to support them also expanded. Over 16 million animals served during the First World War alone. They faced the same dangers as their owners. The Royal Society for the Prevention of Cruelty to Animals (RSPCA) has said that almost half a million animals were killed by enemy action, disease or accident during the First World War.

250,000 pigeons helped during the Second World War, many of which were used by the Royal Air Force (RAF) as a back up to radio equipment, and to fly with aircrews in case their aircraft crashed. New jobs emerged for animals in the Second World War: dogs' abilities to sniff out hidden mines and to locate wounded people on the battlefield, or in bombed out houses on the home front, made them invaluable.

In 1943 Maria Dickin CBE, founder of the People's Dispensary for Sick Animals (PDSA), introduced the Dickin Medal, also known as the Animals' Victoria Cross. It is awarded to animals serving with the Armed Forces or in Civil Defence units that have displayed outstanding acts of bravery or devotion. The Dickin Medal has been awarded to 32 pigeons, 36 dogs, 5 horses (including one honorary medal for Warrior the horse representing all horses and other animals killed in the First World War), and one ship's cat, called Simon. Other countries also recognise animals for their courage, including the USA which awards the Animals in War & Peace Medal of Bravery.

Murphy the donkey

Murphy was no ordinary donkey: he was a war hero, known for his incredible bravery at the Battle of Gallipoli during the First World War. Murphy worked tirelessly on the rocky hills with Private John Simpson Kirkpatrick, a stretcher bearer for the Australian and New Zealand Army Corps. Simpson knew with the help of Murphy he could rescue wounded men more quickly. Murphy had the special job of carrying injured soldiers on his sturdy back, taking them to makeshift hospitals where they could get better. He wore a white band with a red cross so that the enemy knew not to injure him or Simpson. Their work was very dangerous though, and Simpson was killed while helping a soldier. Despite the loss of his friend, Murphy continued to climb down the hill, determined to bring the soldier in his care back to safety. Murphy was later awarded the RSPCA Purple Cross for his unwavering courage.

OPPOSITE
Cher Ami the pigeon

With a flap of his wings, Cher Ami soared through the sky, dodging as many bullets as possible, in a race against time. The trenches were full of danger, and it wasn't long before a bullet whizzing by hit him. He began to tumble to the ground, but this wouldn't stop him! Onwards he flew — he had to deliver the life-saving message secured to his leg. Cher Ami belonged to a battalion of American soldiers based in northern France during the First World War. He was Major Charles Whittlesey's last hope. Caught behind enemy lines, Whittlesey needed to alert headquarters to his battalion's position. He sent Cher Ami, who amazingly delivered the note despite being badly injured. A rescue party was despatched, and Whittlesey's battalion were saved. Cher Ami was awarded the French Croix de Guerre and the Animals in War & Peace Medal of Bravery.

NEXT PAGE
Tirpitz the pig

As the German cruiser SMS *Dresden* sunk into the Pacific Ocean, two little pink ears bobbed along the surface. Sailors of HMS *Glasgow* looked ahead in surprise. To their amazement, it was a pig! They pulled her from the water with much difficulty. She made a mighty impression on the sailors, and they decided to keep her on board as a mascot, naming her Tirpitz, after Alfred von Tirpitz, the Grand Admiral of the German Imperial Navy during the First World War.

Sergeant Bill the goat

With a shaggy coat and a twinkle in his eyes, Sergeant Bill was the mascot of the 5th Infantry Battalion of the Canadian Expeditionary Force during the First World War. He spent much of his time making mischief, nibbling important documents and sneaking beer from the canteen! But his antics saved the day: hearing the high-pitched whine of an incoming shell, Bill jumped into action – headbutting three soldiers one by one into a nearby trench. The soldiers landed with a thud but were soon grateful for their bumps and bruises when a shell exploded close by moments later. Without Bill's expert hearing, the soldiers would have been killed. After the war, Bill was awarded the 1914–15 Star, the British War Medal and the Victory Medal.

Dromedary camels

Dromedary camels were ideal companions during the desert campaigns of the First World War. They were able to carry heavy loads, survive the scorching heat and go without water for days on end. They were fitted with wicker and canvas stretchers called cacolets to carry wounded men to hospital.

Fox cub mascot

Animals had many important jobs during wartime — some were used for their incredible abilities, like hauling heavy loads, helping the wounded and alerting soldiers to incoming dangers, others also served as official mascots, wearing special uniforms and taking part in ceremonies. The fox cub mascot of RAF No. 32 Squadron would have brought much comfort during the difficult moments of the First World War.

OPPOSITE

Togo the cat

Sailors have welcomed cats on board ships since ancient times. Their clever rat-catching skills and snuggly nature make them perfect mascots. It was increasingly popular to keep cats on ships during wartime, and many became famous, like Togo here. Togo, a Persian cat, lived on board HMS *Dreadnaught* and was well-known for hiding in the barrels of the ship's main battery gun.

NEXT PAGE

Warrior the horse

Full of courage, Warrior charged into battle at Moreuil Wood, his hooves pounding as the rattle of bullets and the whine of shells crashed around him. He stayed calm in the face of danger, with his unflinching bravery giving much courage to the soldiers around him. Over four long years, Warrior, alongside his distinguished owner and rider Jack Seely, a Brigadier, galloped into some of the fiercest moments of the First World War. Having seen action during the first day of the Battle of the Somme, and with a narrow escape at the Battle of Passchendaele after being buried in deep mud, he truly earned the name Warrior. In 2014 Warrior's heroic nature was recognised and he was awarded the PDSA Dickin Medal.

Rip the Terrier

During the Blitz, when London was hit by heavy bombing from the Luftwaffe, Rip and his handler, Air Raid Precautions warden E King, would rush to the scene of bombed-out buildings. They would work carefully through the rubble, searching for survivors. Rip wasn't trained as a search-and-rescue dog, but as a Terrier-cross, he was naturally good at finding people. He saved the lives of over 100 people and won the PDSA Dickin Medal for bravery.

Cow

During the Second World War, nightly blackouts were introduced to protect people as much as possible from bombing raids. Turning off the lights made it harder for enemy planes to find and attack Britain's towns and cities. The dark nights also made it much more difficult to see, and car accidents caused the deaths of many people and animals during the early part of the war. Some cows were even painted with white stripes so that they could be seen by people and motorists at night!

Bill the Bull Terrier

Bill, a Bull Terrier, lived on board the battlecruiser HMS *Hood* during the Second World War. He was their unofficial mascot and belonged to the ship's padre, Reverend Harold Beardmore. As the ship sailed through rough seas and tense battles, Bill brought joy and comfort to the sailors. HMS *Hood* was lost in 1941, but luckily both Bill and his owner were transferred off the ship shortly before it sunk in action.

Bandoola the elephant

Bandoola, a large and playful elephant, lived in the tropical jungles of Burma, hauling heavy logs from the timber plantations. In 1942 Japan invaded Burma, and Bandoola and other elephants helped the Allies move much-needed supplies away from enemy lines. With the Japanese troops advancing closer and closer, it was no longer safe for the elephants and the local women and children to stay in Burma. The closest route to safety was through India, but a 100-foot cliff blocked their passage. It was too steep for the elephants to climb. Slowly and painfully the unit carved steps into the cliff, just large enough for elephant feet! With enemy fire in earshot, at last the steps were finished. Bandoola and the other elephants carefully made the arduous climb up the cliff. It took them three long hours to reach the top, but finally they made it!

OPPOSITE

Scrappy the dog & **Joe** the monkey

Scrappy the dog and Joe the monkey were mascots of the 390th Bomb Group, US Eighth Air Force. Joe would climb onto Scrappy's back and together they would race around the airfield. Their adventures continued in the skies with the crew of the B-17 Flying Fortress *Honey Chile*. They would join the crew on missions, bringing comfort and fun during tense moments. By the end of the war, they had earned many flying hours and became popular aviation mascots.

NEXT PAGE

Chips the dog

As the sun rose over Sicily, the soldiers of the 3rd Infantry Division waded ashore with Chips the sentry dog at their side, ready to advance inland. The soldiers waited patiently for the right moment to make their move, but Chips had his own idea. Racing ahead, he ran like lightening down the beach towards the hut where an Italian machine-gunner was firing. The soldiers roared at him to 'STOP', but Chips continued, all the more determined. Fearless, he caught the machine-gunner in his jaws, forcing him to surrender. Four other Italian soldiers followed close behind, waving their arms above their heads in surrender. Later that evening, Chip's powerful nose scouted ten hidden Italian soldiers. He was awarded a number of medals, including the PDSA Dickin Medal for animal bravery and the American Distinguished Service Cross, Silver Star and Purple Heart.

Wojtek the bear

Wojtek the bear was found as a cub by Polish soldiers in Iran and was cared for by them throughout the Second World War. He travelled with the soldiers through Egypt and Italy, getting into much trouble along the way. As a large and strong bear, he would help his unit by carrying heavy boxes of artillery shells. He also had a voracious appetite, eating oodles of cereal, biscuits, bread, marmalade and fruit, all stolen from the soldiers' rations. His particular favourite was honey. One day, ravenously hungry, Wojtek snuck into the camp's food stores and raided the shelves. He pawed at oil, knocked down shelves and created a huge mess. With golden honey dripping from his huge paws, Wojtek was caught red-handed. The greedy bear's kind spirit and playfulness was much loved by the soldiers and his naughty behaviour was soon forgiven.

Olga the reindeer

Olga the reindeer found herself on board HMS *Belfast* as an unexpected gift from the Soviet Northern Fleet Commander, Admiral Arseny Golovko. She was housed in one of the former seaplane hangars on the ship, where planes like the Supermarine Walrus were once stored. As HMS *Belfast* sailed through the icy waters of the Arctic campaign, Olga saw the sinking of the German battleship KMS *Scharnhorst* on 26 December 1943.

Antis the German Shepherd

Antis, a scared and frail puppy, was cowering in an abandoned farmhouse in northern France when he was found by downed air gunner Václav Bozděch and injured pilot Pierre Duval. Antis approached the airmen cautiously, looking up at them with big, hopeful eyes. Sensing his hunger, the airmen shared their chocolate and water with Antis, who wagged his tail in delight. The two airmen made their way to leave, aware of the long journey ahead to cross no man's land... But Antis howled with all his might, longing to stay with his new-found friends. Fearing his loud howling would give them away, they swooped Antis up and took him with them. Antis went on to have many adventures with an RAF Czech Squadron, eventually becoming the mascot for No. 311 RAF Squadron, based near Liverpool. Together with Václav, Antis completed 30 missions and received the PDSA Dickin Medal for animal bravery in 1949.

OPPOSITE
Home front horses

During the Second World War, horses had important jobs on the home front. They worked hard on farms with the Women's Land Army, helping plough fields to grow vegetables and grains to feed everyone. They also pulled wagons filled with food and supplies, making sure towns and cities had everything they needed.

NEXT PAGE
Jet the German Shepherd

In late 1944, Germany resumed its bombing of London in a campaign that became known as 'the baby Blitz'. London was once again illuminated by searchlights and abuzz with the wailing sounds of air raid sirens. One night, a hotel shook from the impact of the bombing. The building crumbled, trapping people beneath the rubble. Wardens of the Air Raid Precautions Services set to work to find as many people as possible, with Jet the search-and-rescue dog at their side. His keen nose worked tirelessly, and his wagging tail and excited barks guided the rescuers to those in need. After 12 hours, the wardens decided to call it a day, but Jet would not move... He was certain someone was still trapped. Trusting Jet's instincts, they continued to search, eventually finding a woman caught underneath the fallen beams and shattered bricks. Luckily, she survived, and Jet saved another life. Together, Jet and Corporal Wardle helped save the lives of more than 50 people trapped by the bombing. He was awarded the PDSA Dickin Medal for his valiant service.

Winkie the pigeon

Returning from a mission in Norway, the crew of an RAF Bristol Beaufort bomber came under enemy fire and crashed into the cold and voracious North Sea. They escaped into their life raft and awaited rescue. The bomber had another passenger: Winkie the pigeon. She wriggled free from her cage moments before the aircraft sank. Flying with all of her might, she headed for home and arrived hours later: cold, wet and her feathers clogged with oil. Her owner, George Ross, immediately realised she'd been aboard an aircraft and alerted the nearest RAF base at Leuchars in Scotland. A search-and-rescue aircraft took to the skies and within 15 minutes spotted the life raft out at sea. All crew were safely rescued and were home by the afternoon. Winkie was one of the first animals to receive the PDSA Dickin Medal for animal bravery.

Sheila the Sheepdog

On a cold, wintry evening, thick with snow, Sheila the Sheepdog was heading home with her owner, when the sound of a B-17 Flying Fortress overhead caught their attention. Suddenly, there came a loud BANG. It was clear the aircraft had crashed. Rushing ahead, Sheila scrambled up the hillside to the site of the wreckage. With her sharp sense of smell, she quickly found four airmen and barked loudly to catch her owner John Dagg and local shepherd Frank Moscrop's attention. One of the airmen was badly injured and needed first aid. With Sheila's help, they were led down the hillside to safety. As they reached home, the crashed aircraft exploded with a thunderous BOOM. Luckily, Sheila had found the airmen in the nick of time. John and Frank received the British Empire Medal for their bravery, and Sheila was awarded the PDSA Dickin Medal. She was the first non-military dog to receive this honour.

Swabby the puppy

Swabby the puppy joined his owner, sailor
Edward Hutton, in an invasion craft heading
for the Allied landings in Normandy, France,
on D-Day. To keep Swabby safe, the crew of
Hutton's ship made him a special life preserver.

Venus the Bulldog

During the Second World War, Venus, a proud Bulldog, was the mascot of the destroyer HMS *Vansittart*. She belonged to the captain of the ship, Lieutenant Commander Richard Lindsay Stephen Gaisford. She entertained the crew and cheered their spirits during stressful operations. Bulldogs like Venus were very popular during wartime, as many believed they looked similar to Prime Minister Winston Churchill!

Barbara the polar bear

In the chilly waters of Greenland, Barbara, a tiny polar bear cub, drifted all alone on an iceberg. A Royal Navy light cruiser was on patrol close by, and it wasn't long before naval officers spotted the cub, in much need of warmth and food! Scooping her up, Barbara became a much-loved guest and mascot on board the ship. But Barbara grew and grew, soon becoming too big for her new home! She was no longer a small cub, but a large and powerful polar bear. Her companions decided to take to the Royal Navy's training facility on Whale Island, where a zoo had been set up to look after retired mascots.

Kitten in hammock

Mascots were much-loved by their companions
and crews would often create unique items
for their furry friends. This ship's cat was made
a special hammock to rest in on board the
aircraft carrier HMS *Eagle*.

Salvo the paradog

Salvo was the first dog in the United States Air Force in Britain to become a paradog! Training to be a dispatch carrier for Lieutenant Hugh Fletcher, he would practise parachute jumping from huge heights at an airfield in Essex. He had the important job of carrying messages for the Allies when radios stopped working or weren't available.

Simon the cat

Simon the cat lived on board HMS *Amethyst* during the Chinese Civil War. His fur was jet black with spots of white on his nose and chest, and his green eyes sparkled with mischief. But Simon wasn't mischievous in a naughty way; he was a hero in his own feline fashion. Simon had a special duty: he was the ship's chief ratcatcher. Rats were a huge problem on ships; they gnawed through food supplies and spread disease. After each successful mission, Simon would proudly leave his catch on a sailor's bed as a gift – much to their horror! Later in the war, HMS *Amethyst* was struck by Chinese fighters as it sailed on a mission up the Yangtze River to the Chinese town of Nanking. 56 of the crew died, but luckily Simon survived. He was awarded the PDSA Dickin Medal for his bravery.

DRAW YOUR OWN ANIMALS

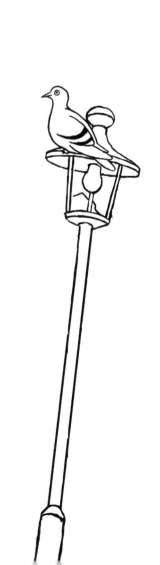